Benjamin A. Blundon

Atlantic City as a Winter Resort

Benjamin A. Blundon

Atlantic City as a Winter Resort

ISBN/EAN: 9783337253363

Printed in Europe, USA, Canada, Australia, Japan

Cover: Foto ©Andreas Hilbeck / pixelio.de

More available books at **www.hansebooks.com**

ATLANTIC CITY

AS A

WINTER RESORT

Comprising Meteorological Statistics concerning Temperature, Humidity, Amount of Rainfall, etc.; Compiled from Official Reports and Local Observations of the United States Signal Service.

Also the Sanitary and Social Features of Atlantic City; its Hotels and Other Attractions; Testimonials of Prominent Physicians as to the Value of the Climate; Suggestions to Invalids regarding Hygiene, etc., etc.

B. A. BLUNDON,
Sergeant Signal Service, U.S.A.

PHILADELPHIA:
LINEAWEAVER AND WALLACE, PRINTERS,
No. 32 South Fourth Street.

PREFACE.

The following pamphlet includes the most important matter contained in one written a few years ago by a well-known physician of Atlantic City. It embraces also a fuller account of the town itself—its hotels, water supply, drainage, sailing, fishing, objects of interest, drives and other attractions for tourists and pleasure-seekers, as well as for invalids. The tables and other meteorological statistics have been carefully gone over by me and supplemented in several instances by the figures of more recent years. They are drawn from the official records of the War Department and of the Signal Station here. I am indebted to several persons and particularly to Mr. John F. Hall, of the Atlantic City *Times*, for assistance in preparing this work.

B. A. BLUNDON.

United States Signal Station,
Atlantic City, N. J.,
February 28th, 1885.

ATLANTIC CITY

AS A

WINTER RESORT.

THE growing fashion of visiting coast resorts in winter is of European origin, but has already taken a firm hold in the United States. In England and other transatlantic countries, the great benefits derived from a change of climate during the winter and spring have long been recognized by physicians, and the growth of winter health resorts has been a natural consequence.

In this country, till recently, Florida has been the principal refuge for invalids during the cold season. Its great distance, however, from the large cities and centres of population in the North has prevented many from availing themselves of its advantages. Atlantic City, New Jersey, is vastly more accessible, and offers many attractions as a winter resort.

This place had long since achieved fame as a summer residence, its fine beach affording excellent bathing, its remarkably dry and bracing air attracting throngs of invalids and convalescents, and its proximity and extraordinary railroad facilities further contributing to its rapid growth and popularity. The doctors gradually became aware of the fact that the marked healing qualities of the air were as active and efficient in winter as in summer. It was discovered also that so far from being colder here in winter than in Philadelphia and other neighboring cities, it was actually warmer upon the average, and very decidedly so during the prevalence of a sea breeze.

Apart from climatic considerations, the city itself has many interesting features. It is a regularly laid out and handsomely built city with a permanent population of eight thousand. All the essentials of city life are at hand. There are miles of beautiful streets, stores of all kinds, street cars in constant operation, schools, churches, circulating libraries, and excellent markets, which make it a city in fact as well as in name. Many of the hotels have been constructed in the most modern style and furnished with every appliance necessary for comfort in summer or winter. Open grates, steam radiators and stoves maintain an uniform temperature; all the surroundings are bright and cheerful. The hotels are located on the ocean side of the town. From glass-enclosed sun galleries invalid visitors may enjoy the magnificent prospect and promenade, safe from too great exposure upon the colder winter days.

One's enjoyment of out-door exercise is all that could be desired, from walking, sailing or driving in the pure bracing air. The Inlet is the rendezvous of those who have a penchant for sailing, gunning or fishing. A broad plank walk skirts the whole ocean front of the town for two miles or more, so that pedestrians may watch the chasing billows while they take their constitutionals with dry feet.

At low tide a splendid ocean drive extends down the strand past Chelsea Beach, a new and very exclusive suburb, and the Elephant Bazaar at South Atlantic to Longport, at the southern extremity, a distance of ten miles. A longer drive is across the bridge and meadow turnpike to the mainland. There a smooth country road extends a dozen miles or more from Leed's Point above to Somers' Point below, through thriving villages, past attractive country homes, overlooking charming meadow and ocean scenery.

ABSENCE OF MALARIA.

The following extract from a medical article,* quoted in the pamphlet previously referred to, is important testimony as to the absence of malaria here:

"The sandy beaches on the New Jersey coast are generally free from malaria, except at points where freshwater streams empty into the ocean. Professor Alfred L. Loomis, of New York, in a recent lecture, discussed the subject of malaria with his accustomed ability. He said: 'Salt-water marshes are, as a rule, especially free from malaria; but mix salt and fresh water, as on some of the New Jersey marshes, and you have the conditions for generating the poison. Marshes that rest on a substratum of sand are not so malarial as those that rest on limestone, clay, or mud.'

"Atlantic City, which, by reason of its rapid growth and prominence among health resorts, is now attracting to an unusual degree the critical attention of sanitarians, is fortunate in being surrounded by a plenitude of unmixed salt water, and in being founded upon the driest of sand. So far, therefore, as concerns malaria, that subtle, intangible poison, which defies alike the microscope and the reagents of the chemist, but produces in some unknown way the periodical fevers, Atlantic City seems to be highly favored. Intermittent and remittent are strangers to the regular residents, and it is the constant experience of malarial patients coming here that they obtain rapid relief

---

* " The Sanitary Condition of our Sea-shore Health Resorts," by Boardman Reed, M. D., *Medical and Surgical Reporter*, July 9, 1881, page 54.

with far less medication than at home, often especially in the case of children, with no medication at all."

WATER SUPPLY AND DRAINAGE.

Atlantic City now has a two-fold water supply. Nearly every house has a cemented cistern or wooden tank in which water distilled from the clouds is preserved pure and sweet for use when required. When carefully kept, and especially when filtered, rain water is entirely reliable, and usually affords an adequate supply for drinking and culinary purposes.

But water works of the most elaborate character were built, and spring water introduced from the mainland, seven miles distant, in June, 1882. A standpipe 135 feet high, having a capacity of 500,000 gallons, ensures at all times an abundant supply for every purpose, including the sprinkling of streets and extinguishing of fires.

This place promises to be hereafter the best drained city on the Atlantic coast. Years ago provision was made for getting rid of the surface water, and since the compulsory filling up of low lots, there has been little ground for complaint in this respect. All garbage has long been and still is removed daily in closely covered barrels. Other refuse and excreta have for some years past been stored temporarily in carefully constructed vaults with excellent ventilating arrangements, in the case of the leading hotels, and removed at frequent intervals entirely beyond the city limits during the latter part of the night usually, and by the odorless excavator apparatus.

An improved system of underground sewerage, adopted by the Board of Health and City Council after a very careful study of various rival plans, is now assured to the town. Work was begun upon this in the fall of 1883, and is now, under the direction of a New York company, progressing rapidly toward completion. Early in the present season (1885) it is expected to be in operation.

By this system the sewage flows through straight pipes to a central reservoir. It is thence pumped several miles away and there filtered by a patent process, the solid portions being converted into phosphates by the addition of certain chemicals, and the purified liquid permitted to empty into an arm of the sea behind the town.

A similar system has for some years been in successful operation at Pullman, near Chicago, Ill., where, with less grades than have been provided for Atlantic City, it has given the utmost satisfaction. Without such a comprehensive method, including a pumping station and the filtering process, the flat beaches of the New Jersey coast cannot, in the opinion of good sanitary authorities, be successfully and safely drained. To empty the crude sewage into the ocean, as is done at some seacoast towns, is objectionable in many ways.

A STUDY OF THE CLIMATE FROM THE PHYSICIAN'S STANDPOINT.

The following is a reproduction with some necessary emendations of an article contributed by Dr. Boardman Reed to the Philadelphia *Medical Times* of December 18, 1880, entitled "Winter Health Resorts; The Climate of Atlantic City and its effects on Pulmonary Diseases." It was subsequently reprinted, together with several other medical articles by the same writer, in a pamphlet entitled "Atlantic City as a Winter Health Resort," numerous copies of which were sent to physicians in the northern cities. The tables have been carefully verified and extended so as to bring them more nearly down to date.

"Where shall we send our invalids for a change of air in winter? This is a practical question which is becoming, year by year, more important to busy physicians, particularly in the great cities of the North. There are certain chronic diseases for which a pure and invigorating air, and especially a climate which will tempt the patients out of doors, are highly desirable. For many cases a change to such an air offers the best hope of cure, or even of amelioration.

"Florida has been much in vogue lately as a winter-resort, and undoubtedly suits numerous patients well; but it is too far away, involving a long and tiresome journey. The distance from home and friends, and the impossibility of conferring in an emergency with the usual medical attendant, are serious inconveniences, and the warm and enervating character of the Southern climate unfits it for a large class of diseases altogether.

"Colorado and Minnesota are even farther away, and their climates, however tonic and useful, are so cold that invalids there can live very little out of doors during the winter; and if they are to be kept prisoners in close heated rooms it might almost as well be in their own homes.

"Atlantic City, New Jersey, a place most favorably located as regards convenience of access, being ninety minutes' ride from Philadelphia by the West Jersey and Camden and Atlantic Railroads, and only four hours from New York by the Pennsylvania Railroad and its branch lines, possesses certain physical advantages which are well worth considering. It has been twenty years or more since physicians began sending patients here in winter. First only now and then a courageous invalid ventured here at this season, but their numbers steadily increased. The experiment proved so successful in hastening the convalescence from acute disease, in improving a large class of chronic affections, and especially in arresting numerous cases of incipient as well as confirmed consumption, that within the last few years the travel to the place in winter has reached very considerable proportions, and the numerous thoroughly heated winter hotels—some of which are as sumptuously furnished and as luxuriously conducted as the leading houses at the summer-resorts—are crowded with invalids, convalescents, and wearied society people through all the months from February on.

"Actual experience has demonstrated that sea air is as valuable in winter as in summer. It also bears out the statistics which prove that the climate of Atlantic City is superior to that of most sea-coast towns, being drier, more equable, and, considering the latitude, unusually mild.

"The city is situated in latitude 39° 22', on an island ten miles long and averaging about half a mile wide. This is separated from the mainland at either end by broad bays or inlets, which are connected by a narrow arm of the sea called 'The Thoroughfare.' There is no body of fresh water nearer than the Delaware river, distant about sixty miles, and the salt-water bays to the landward side are nearly always open, ice seldom forming, except for a short time occasionally in the severest winters.

"Another peculiarity of the location is that all the winds from the landward must pass for long distances—hundreds of miles in some directions—over a very dry and porous sandy soil, upon which snow rarely lies for any time. These winds, including those from the north, north-west, west, and south-west, are therefore to some extent both dried and warmed in their passage.

"INFLUENCE OF THE GULF STREAM.

"Though the coast of Southern New Jersey has a general direction from north-east to south-west, the beach at Atlantic City trends more to the westward, so that it faces almost directly southward. Therefore south as well as east winds are sea breezes here, and both blow across the Gulf Stream, which, by the way, exercises considerable influence upon the climate of this part of the coast.

"Mr. C. P. Patterson, Superintendent of the United States Coast and Geodetic Survey Office at Washington has kindly furnished me with a large map indicating accurately the course of the Gulf Stream, and with some interesting facts concerning it.

"This map shows at a glance that the heated waters of the tropics, pouring through the space between Cuba and Florida, flow in a north-easterly direction along the coast of Georgia and the Carolinas, diffusing themselves as they go, until from a compact stream less than fifty miles wide, they have become opposite Chesapeake Bay a broad expanse upwards of four hundred miles in width. This really includes numerous parallel or slightly diverging currents of very warm water with overflow currents of a somewhat lower temperature. One of these overflow currents approaches within sixty-five miles of Atlantic City, while it is one hundred and ten miles from Sandy Hook. The principal current is farther away, being one hundred and thirty-five miles from Atlantic City, one hundred and eighty-five miles from Sandy Hook, and about the same distance from Long Branch and Montauk Point.

"But the exceptional mildness of this climate may be attributed to the peculiar course of the Gulf Stream in this vicinity as much as to its proximity. The innermost current, according to the map received from the Coast Survey office, has a direction opposite Atlantic City of east-north-east, but turns more and more to the eastward till in latitude 40°—that of Philadelphia—it bears nearly due east. The main current turns more abruptly, and a little north of latitude 38°, some distance to the southward of Atlantic City, has a course directly eastward. Our south, south-east, and east winds, then, must all pass for three hundred to five hundred miles at least over more or less heated water which has come directly from the Gulf of Mexico. Our only ocean breezes not affected in this way are those from the northeast. But for places farther up the coast, particularly those north of latitude 40°, the case is different. Neither their north-east nor east winds can be appreciably modified by the Gulf Stream. Their south and south-east winds may be favorably influenced to some extent, but less than are the same winds at Atlantic City, since they pass over a much larger surface of cold water after crossing the Gulf Stream.

METEOROLOGICAL STATISTICS.

Temperature, Humidity and Barometrical Pressure at Atlantic City, New Jersey.

Months, 1880.	Mean Temperature.	Range of Temperature.		Mean Humidity.	Mean Barometer.
		Max	Min.		
January	41.1	64	13	79.3	30.189
February	38.2	71	11	74.4	30.129
March	40.1	72	18	71.9	30.061
Months, 1881.					
February	30.3			83.8	30.173
March	38.4			74.6	29.735
Months, 1882.					
February	37.9	53.7	20.3	78.5	30.139
March	41.4	65.5	21.	73.5	30.077

"The mean temperature for January, February, March, and December, the four coldest months of the year, was, in 1879, 34.7°; in 1878, 36.8°; and in 1877, 35.9°.

"The prevailing winds in winter are those from the west and northwest, which are usually dry and bracing. The east and south winds, which often blow for days at a time, are warmer and more humid. North-east winds, which are unpleasant, usually prevail for two or three days at the time of the equinoctial storms, but are infrequent during the remainder of the year.

"Observations taken at my office, in the centre of the town, at 7 A. M., 12 M., and 6 and 10 P. M., show that in December, 1879, there were twenty-six days during which the thermometer did not fall below 32°, the freezing point; also that there were only two days in the same month when the thermometer did not indicate at noon a temperature above 40°; and that there were ten days upon which it was not below 50° at the same hour. During the January following (1880) there were twenty-four days during which the mercury never fell below the freezing point at any hour, and only two days during which it went below 30°. It was only once in the same month lower than 40° at noon, and only three times lower than 45° at the same hour. On nineteen of the thirty-one days the thermometer stood at 50° or above at mid-day.

"These mid-day temperatures are obviously more important than averages, for it is in the daytime that invalids take their airing out of doors.

Annual Amount of Rainfall in Inches at the Principal Cities and Stations on the Atlantic Coast for the years ended June 30, 1878, 1879, 1880, 1881, 1882. Also the Mean Annual Amount since the Stations were Established.

Station.	1878.	1879.	1880.	1881.	1882.	Mean annual amount since Establishment of Station.	
Atlantic City, N. J.	42.90	40.65	44.23	55.48	39.55	40.24	8 years.
Barnegat, N. J.	52.35	49.38	47.27	60.13	58.85	50.20	8 "
Cape May, N. J.	47.99	42.44	50.92	60.54	40.41	46.70	10 "
Charleston, S. C.	68.62	64.33	44.47	48.80	48.63	60.91	11 "
Jacksonville, Fla.	52.11	51.62	54.99	66.87	48.69	55.74	10 "
Newport, R. I.	55.84	52.20	40.75	61.45	44.52	59.98	6 "
New Orleans, La.	73.31	58.29	60.84	67.33	58.22	65.63	11 "
New York City	42.68	43.68	33.24	49.50	35.60	42.67	11 "
Norfolk, Va.	66.28	44.44	34.54	54.48	46.49	51.43	11 "
Portland, Me.	45.61	41.10	38.24	45.02	42.99	39.33	10 "
Sandy Hook, N. J.	54.86	60.37	46.75	53.14	46.20	52.05	8 "
Wilmington, N. C.	84.12	50.90	50.13	53.35	46.56	57.28	11 "

This table of rainfall as enlarged by making it cover a series of five years, shows that Portland, Me., alone of all the cities and stations mentioned, had during that period a less rainfall than Atlantic City. This is an extraordinary fact. Atlantic City has less rainfall than other resorts on the coast so far as the official records show, and has thus a strong basis for its claim to exceptional dryness.

"The dryness of this climate, as compared with other seaside resorts, is best shown by the statistics of the rainfall, which is less here than at any other place on the coast, as appears from the foregoing table. The readings of the hygrometers at the different stations are not so significant, since at some of them, including Atlantic City, the instruments are located so near to the beach, and at so low an elevation above the sea level (less than thirteen feet here) as to be affected by the spray, during strong winds off the water, and by occasional morning mists, which do not extend back into the town.

Annual Amount of Wind in Miles at Various Stations for a Series of Five Years.

Stations.	1880.	1881.	1882.	1883.	1884.	Average Yearly Amount.
Atlantic City, N. J. . .	87.070	83.581	86.498	80.769	75.232	82.630
Barnegat City, N. J. . .	126.718	116.642	117.564	128.934	125.081	122.988
Cape May, N. J. . . .	134.455	129.755	123.041	128.330	134.584	130.055
Sandy Hook, N. J. . .	124.278	108.471	122.601			118.450

This wind table is a new one entirely. A foot-note at this point in the former pamphlet mentioned briefly the figures showing that during the year 1879 there was very much less wind at Atlantic City than at the neighboring stations on either side. The above table shows in a striking manner by the statistics of five years that there is on the average greatly less wind here than at any station on the New Jersey coast. This is especially important as bearing upon the fitness of the place as a winter resort, since high winds in winter mean trying weather, and the less the velocity of the wind, other things being equal, the safer and more enjoyable is exercise out of doors.

"After all, however, it is with climates as with medicines,—trustworthy evidence as to what they have accomplished is the most valuable. With regard to nervous, rheumatic, gouty, dyspeptic, and various other chronic ailments (including most of those peculiar to women), which are usually found to be benefited here in the summer, equal benefit may be expected in the winter. Convalescents from acute disease, or from surgical operations, nearly always improve remarkably upon being removed to this place from the large cities.

"As to diseases of the respiratory organs, I have had personal knowledge of many patients suffering from various forms of such affections who have made trials of this climate in winter. The bronchial and laryngeal cases have, as a rule, improved, some of them very decidedly, though there have been exceptions. The consumptives who were in the third stage, or in any stage with evidences of actively progressing disease of the lung and decided hectic, have only exceptionally been benefited. Those, however, in the pretubercular or incipient stage, and those even in the advanced stages where the destructive process has been advancing slowly, have often experienced very marked improvement. In a considerable proportion of the cases of these latter classes the disease has been apparently arrested, and some of them seem to be cured.

" Detailed reports of the cases I have treated at Atlantic City would fully bear out the foregoing general conclusions, but would unduly extend this paper and necessitate the exclusion of several reports I have received from prominent Philadelphia physicians concerning the effect of this climate upon their patients, in winter especially. Some of these physicians have been sending patients hither for more than twenty years. Their testimony is more valuable than mine, and can not be impugned on the ground of partiality.

" It is a significant fact that pneumonia and bronchitis are of infrequent origin here, and when they do occur the patients *almost invariably recover*. I have not known an uncomplicated attack of either disease to prove fatal.

REPORTS FROM PHYSICIANS.

" The reports from physicians above referred to were received in response to inquiries recently sent to them. Many others wrote brief apologies, not having the notes or the leisure to tabulate the results of their experience as I had requested. Only one physician objected to the climate either for bronchitis or early phthisis.

" Dr. Laurence Turnbull writes : ' The number of cases of phthisis that I have sent to Atlantic City have been few *in the last stages*, as I found they were not improved by a residence at the seashore, dry even as it is,' adding that a few cases in those stages were aggravated, but goes on to say, ' I have been much pleased with its influence on the first stages of phthisis, asthma, laryngitis, bronchitis, and nasal catarrh, when all ordinary means have failed in the city, by causing improvement in the appetite, assisting the digestion, and giving a healthier tone to the skin. In convalescence from catarrhal pneumonia and typhoid fever the results have been most gratifying. In certain forms of *otitis media purulenta* I do *not* find the air of Atlantic very beneficial, and in many cases diseases of the ear are caused by exposure of that organ to the waves. In strumous diseases of eyes, joints, limbs, etc., I have found the change to Atlantic City, if persisted in for several seasons, of permanent benefit.'

" Dr. Thomas J. Yarrow writes: ' It has not been my practice, as a rule, to advise patients suffering with tuberculous and other diseases of the respiratory passages to sojourn at the seaside. Exceptionally, I have had them go to Atlantic City, and have known cases of incipient phthisis, chronic bronchitis, asthma, and laryngitis to improve in that location. My experience of late is inducing me to recommend a larger number of such cases to reside at Atlantic City.'

" Dr. Thomas G. Morton thus bears testimony: ' I have been in the habit of sending to the shore at Atlantic City many patients, more especially surgical cases, but a large number also of those with lung affections, and especially those having a (hereditary) tubercular disposition, and I think especially such cases have been vastly benefited by the sojourn.'

"Dr. James Darrach, of Germantown, writes: 'Have sent several cases of autumnal catarrh to Atlantic City, and think without exception they were benefited, two of them being certainly exempt from these attacks while at the shore. The only case of slow convalescence from pneumonia died at Atlantic City. This was about twenty-three years ago. A case of obstinate general bronchitis was cured in about ten days. A case of what I supposed to be tubercular laryngitis was very much benefited, and subsequently recovered. I have also had other cases of obstinate catarrh which returned well after a sojourn at Atlantic City.'

"Dr. Eugene P. Bernardy reports as follows: 'With but one exception, all my cases of phthisis, both in the early and late stages, amounting to twelve in all, have been decidedly benefited by a sojourn at Atlantic City, and one case positively cured,—that is, as far as human ear can ascertain. Of the three cases of convalescence from pneumonia all were decidedly benefited. In a child suffering from chronic pneumonia the lung in a few weeks was almost entirely cleared up. In bronchial affections (chronic) I have seen no permanent benefit in any of the six cases I have sent there; all benefited while at the seashore, but a few months after their return relapsed. The case of phthisis cured had been examined by myself and Dr. Hall in Philadelphia, and while at the seashore examined by Dr. L. Turnbull. We all diagnosed incipient phthisis. This was nearly six years ago. On her return she had gained forty pounds, and has remained well ever since.'

"Dr. John H. Packard says, referring to Atlantic City, 'I can only say that I frequently advise convalescents to go there, and that it is a very common thing with me to be asked by patients whether it would not do them good to spend a week or two there. I do not now recollect any case that has been wholly without benefit from that climate, and could adduce many that have gained great advantage from it.'

"Dr. D. Murray Cheston writes: 'I cannot say how many cases of pulmonary or bronchial troubles I have sent there, but the general result has been most satisfactory. The cases were all sent in the late winter or early spring months, and have invariably returned improved.'

"Prof. J. M. Da Costa writes briefly as follows: 'I have sent too few patients with pulmonary disease to Atlantic City to have the data to answer your questions. Some who were in a run-down condition and affected with chronic bronchial catarrh did very well.'

"Dr. Ellwood Wilson writes that in the summer months he does not think patients with fully developed phthisis improve by a protracted residence at Atlantic City, but adds, 'During the winter months—say from October to July—I regard it as a very favorable locality for consumptive patients.'

"Dr. R. J. Levis writes that his practice (being almost exclusively surgical) 'is not of a kind to furnish experience with regard to the beneficial influence of Atlantic City in pulmonary affections,' but that he has 'a good opinion of its dry and mild climate.'

"Dr. James J. Levick has not sent any cases of phthisis, but has sent 'several cases of laryngeal and bronchial irritation and one or two cases of hay asthma, which improved greatly while at Atlantic City.' He adds, 'The cases which have derived most benefit, however, and of which I have sent not a few in the late winter months, have been patients after typhoid fever,—patients whose nervous systems have been much disturbed, persons who have needed brain rest, etc.'

"Dr. William H. Bennett, in describing his experience particularly at the Children's Seashore House and at the Seaside House for Invalid Women, says: 'My experience of the effects of a sojourn at Atlantic City upon those suffering from pulmonary diseases has been confined to what I have seen among transient visitors during the summer months of the past seven years. I have had little or no experience of the effects either of a prolonged stay or of a stay in winter. My patients were, with the exception of a majority of those suffering from phthisis, nearly all children. I have had not less than a hundred cases of acute bronchitis, nearly all of which ran a milder and shorter course than similar cases do in Philadelphia. A few, perhaps ten, cases of subacute bronchitis, which had remained stationary in the city for some time, rapidly recovered at the seashore. Three or four cases of chronic bronchitis, with emphysema and occasional severe attacks of asthma, greatly improved; but about an equal number showed no change. Two or three cases of tardy convalescence from pneumonia made much more rapid progress towards recovery after their removal to the seashore. Two cases of empyema with external fistulæ greatly improved. About twenty cases of phthisis have been under my care at Atlantic City. These have been in all stages of the disease. A very few, I recall but three, derived no benefit: all the others improved in general health. In some, even of the advanced cases, the improvement was marked. In many of the cases the cough became less troublesome and the breathing less labored. Nearly all slept better. Hectic frequently disappeared entirely, or was greatly lessened.'"

A DRY AND BRACING CLIMATE.

STRONG LETTERS FROM TWO PROMINENT PHYSICIANS.

Dr. William Pepper's report of his experience in sending patients to Atlantic City was not received until after the original publication of the above article, but was given a place in the former pamphlet. It is emphatic testimony from a recognized authority in pulmonary diseases:

PHILADELPHIA, 1811 Spruce Street.

"MY DEAR DOCTOR REED:—In reply to your question as to my experience with the climate of Atlantic City in cases of diseases of the chest, I would make the following remarks:

"I am more strongly convinced each year of the advantage in the treatment of such cases possessed by dry, bracing climates as compared with moist, sedative climates. Undoubtedly there are certain special types of disease that do better in the latter, but it has seemed to me that the benefit derived amounts to palliation or relief, and not to radical cure. One difficulty attaching to the residence of invalids in dry, bracing climates is the fact that a far greater degree of attention to personal hygiene and systematic regimen is required. There are fewer risks of renewed congestions or increased catarrhs in a moist sedative climate, it is true; but on the other hand, if the patient is carefully instructed by his medical adviser as to the proper mode of living in a dry, bracing climate, and is willing to faithfully attend to all the details of such instructions, there is in my judgment a far higher degree of actual, permanent benefit to be secured in the great majority of cases.

"This applies especially to patients who are still in the curable stage of consumption, for in a large proportion of cases of phthisis there is an early stage when no true tuberculous disease exists, and when a cure is possible under the combined influence of suitable climate, rigidly careful hygiene, and judicious medical treatment.

"I would further say that I have seen enough of the results of the climate at Atlantic City to satisfy me that it acts powerfully in most cases as a dry and bracing climate. Many cases of incipient phthisis, and even phthisis in the second stage, have been greatly and permanently benefited by a residence there under a strict rule of living and treatment. In several cases of chronic pleurisy with marked atony of the skin and system, and retarded absorption of the morbid products, I have seen the removal to Atlantic City soon followed by rapid improvement. I am referring to this climate as I have observed it at all seasons of the year. And in respect particularly to that which I have just mentioned, the element of relaxation of the skin, which is common to so many diseases and is so powerfully conducive to renewed attacks of congestion or inflammation, I have observed excellent results from the stimulating dry air of Atlantic City.

"In retarded convalescence from acute diseases, and in conditions of impaired nervous tone, I have also found its climate very valuable. On the other hand, in the majority of cases of organic heart disease and of bronchial asthma, the results of residence at Atlantic City have not been favorable.

"It is unquestionably an admirable climate, and I am convinced that if those who resort to it would but observe with sufficient patience and minuteness the necessary precautions, they would for the most part avoid the bad effects that some have experienced, and would find it highly beneficial in the conditions I have above mentioned, as well as in others to which I have no time to allude.

"Yours very truly,
"WILLIAM PEPPER.

"Dr. Boardman Reed,
    Atlantic City, N. J."

In commenting on the foregoing letter Dr. Reed said:

"My experience as a resident physician coincides in the main perfectly with that of Dr. Pepper as above recorded; but with regard to asthma, it has happened to me to see a majority of cases do well at Atlantic City, though with some few the climate has manifestly disagreed. One prominent railroad man who suffers much from asthma when inland, spent the whole of last winter here with entire relief."

AN ENTHUSIASTIC TRIBUTE AT AN EARLY DAY.

The following are extracts from a letter written in 1873 by Dr. W. V. Keating, a distinguished Philadelphia physician, to Mr. D. M. Zimmerman:

"Some fifteen years since I visited Atlantic City, and, with many others,* I was struck with the peculiarity of its position, the distinctive characteristics of its climate, the singular dryness of atmosphere, rendering it in many respects one of the most lovely, salubrious climates I have ever visited.

"From careful observations, made for several consecutive years, I have noticed that during the months of June, July, August and September, the prevailing wind at Atlantic City is south by west. Situated in a cove, with a large area of dry, sandy, and thickly timbered land to the south-west, it seems as if the prevailing sea-breeze lost much of its humidity in passing over this thickly-wooded and sandy country, with no fresh water to counteract its effects before reaching the town. The same condition exists also in reference to the northeast winds, which, when they prevail, I have noticed, are much less keen and much less humid than with us, lasting sometimes forty-eight hours at the shore without bringing a drop of rain, whilst at the same time the same wind is attended with great dampness and heavy rain in our city and environs.

"This peculiarly characteristic dryness of the atmosphere and of the sea breezes, however it may be accounted for, is patent to all who have ever sojourned at Atlantic City, and is the distinctive feature

---

* "Among the many eminent medical men who have endorsed my views I am proud to name the late Prof. Jackson, of the University of Pennsylvania, whose farseeing eye and keen judgment caused him, in 1859, to state to me that he considered the atmospheric condition of Atlantic City one of the most peculiar in the country, and that it would, in time, become available in the treatment of many diseases.

of the place to which I attribute its great advantage over every other sea-bathing place on the coast. The time will come when some more exact and satisfactory explanation will be given of the phenomenon, which I now claim as affording to invalids all the invigoration from a seashore residence, without the usually accompanying humidity so aggravating to many diseases.

"This remarkable dryness of climate,* resembling in this respect more the characteristics of Nice, on the Mediterranean, than any seacoast I have ever visited, is the characteristic of the climate of Atlantic City, which affords relief and cure to all cases of rheumatic fever and arthritis, even in the most acute stages. I know of many instances in which invalids, after having recourse, without benefit, to the various mineral waters and baths in the country, have there been entirely cured by a summer sojourn.

"I have ventured to send patients there in the height of an attack of rheumatic gout, in the months of May and June, who have had complete amelioration of all their symptoms within forty-eight hours of their residence, provided they located themselves as near the ocean as possible, so as to avoid the land breezes.

"To another class of cases, also, I am convinced that Atlantic City offers relief, if not positive cure, which cannot be obtained on any other portion of our seacoast. I allude to those trying and refractory cases of chronic bronchitis, laryngitis, incipient tuberculosis, and scrofula. I must add that in the last two years I have been in the habit of sending patients, even in the more advanced stages of tuberculosis and scrofula, with marked benefit. All medical men are familiar with the fact that the above class of cases can seldom venture upon a sojourn at the seaside on account of the dampness, the distinctive feature of such a location, a peculiar condition most apt to aggravate the diseases in question, and considered by some of our best observers as one of the atmospheric conditions most to be feared by those threatened with pulmonary complaints.

"In this respect again Atlantic City offers a striking analogy with Nice, where, it is well known, all the invalids of Europe (affected with chest diseases) flock for a winter's resort.

"It is difficult to estimate the immense advantages resulting to invalids suffering from pulmonary and scrofulous affections, being able to obtain all the benefits accruing from the invigoration and improved digestion of a seaside residence, without the usual pernicious accom-

---

* "In the year 1871 I went to Atlantic City in the month of March, and whilst visiting Mr. Metzger's cottage, on Connecticut Avenue, then close to the ocean, asking to light a cigar, he opened a drawer of a wash-stand and found a lucifer match, which had been there since the cottage had been closed in October. The slightest friction caused it to ignite at once. Visitors are all well conversant with the fact that their wearing apparel never becomes limp under the influence of the sea-breeze, nor their boots and shoes covered with mildew, as in all the other seaside resorts on our coast.

paniment of excessive dampness, which relaxes the system and predisposes to a general catarrhal condition.

". . . . ."

" What a precious boon will it be to the invalids of our country if, without the necessity of exposing themselves to a long sea-voyage, they can find in their own native land all the variations of climate and hygienic conditions conducive to their restoration to health, or the amelioration of their sufferings ! "

FURTHER ADVANTAGES OF ATLANTIC CITY AS A SANITARIUM.

" *Certain partisans of Florida and Minnesota last winter engaged in a spirited controversy concerning the merits of those regions respectively, as resorts for consumptives in winter. Since these climatic extremes were each setting forth its claims so earnestly in the New York *Medical Journal*, it occurred to the writer that the many marked advantages of Atlantic City ought to be placed before the readers of the same publication. Hence an article entitled 'What Atlantic City can do for Consumptives,' was prepared and appeared in the number for March, 1881. The following portions are deemed worthy of being reproduced in this pamphlet :

" It does not seem necessary to decide in favor of either Florida or Minnesota—the extreme south or extreme north—as the only proper residence for such patients in the winter season. Professor Bennett, in his work on ' Pulmonary Consumption,' expresses a sentiment on this point, which, though Dr. Kenworthy has quoted it, appears scarcely to help his case. It is this: ' Now that medical doctrines have changed, that vitalistic and sthenic views of treatment prevail, and are found to give infinitely more satisfactory results than those that followed antiphlogistic treatment, the medical mind in America and Europe looks about for a colder climate. As usual, the pendulum has a tendency to pass to the other extreme ; to go from Madeira, Jamaica, and Barbadoes, from Havana, Florida, and Nassau, to the ice-covered summits of the Swiss mountains, to the frozen plains of Northern America. Many minds can never constitutionally accept and follow the golden adage, " *Medio tutissimus ibis ;* " they cannot remain in the middle of the road ; they must pass from one extreme to the other.'

" Evidently Professor Bennett considers Florida and Minnesota as extremes, and would give the preference to some middle region. Atlantic City, N. J., situated in latitude 39° 22′, is just about midway between the peninsula of Florida and the ' frozen plains of Northern America,' and may therefore claim to be the ' golden mean.' It is

---

* "Atlantic City as a Winter Health Resort," by Boardman Reed, M. D., Philadelphia, 1881.

rapidly growing in favor as a winter resort for many classes of invalids. It has one of the driest and most equable climates on the coast, has better hotel accommodations than can be found in either Florida or Minnesota, and is so accessible to the New England and Middle States that a trip hither is neither a serious undertaking nor a finality involving a complete cutting adrift from home, friends, and physicians, with the prospect of dying among strangers if the climate should not suit.

"There are many patients who are drifting into phthisis as the result of a general break-down following excessive devotion to business or pleasure. These may not care and do not need to expatriate themselves for half the year. They may often do perfectly well at home, provided they avoid all excesses and have the best possible medical treatment; but, their vital forces being at a low ebb, they need occasionally the stimulus to be derived from a few weeks' sojourn in some invigorating seaside climate, where it is not so cold as to keep them in-doors, and yet not so warm as to relax their tissues and still further debilitate them. It is this class of phthisical cases, and numerous other affections resulting from nervous exhaustion, that we see most of here, and find to receive most benefit from the climate.

"Through the courtesy of Sergeant F. B. Garriott, the observer in charge of the signal station in New York, some statistics of the weather in that city during the three spring months of the year 1880 have been obtained, and in the following table are compared with the corresponding figures for Atlantic City, furnished by the observer here:

	Mean Temperature.	Rainfall in Inches.
MARCH, 1880.		
New York City,	34.0	4.66
Atlantic City,	40.1	5.97
APRIL, 1880.		
New York City,	49.0	3.38
Atlantic City,	49.3	1.83
MAY, 1880.		
New York City,	65.0	0.82
Atlantic City,	63.1	0.54

"From this table it will be seen that the temperature during March averaged six degrees higher here than in New York City; in April it was only slightly higher; and in May, when New York began to experience its foretaste of the summer heats, it averaged cooler in Atlantic City. The rainfall was less here in April and May, though a little greater during March, than in New York.

"During the entire year ended June 30th, 1879, the amount of rainfall in New York was 43.68 inches, as against only 40.6 inches at Atlantic City. Taking a series of years, the rainfall in New York City is found to average only a little more than at Atlantic City, though greatly *less* than at most seaside stations. For instance, during the two years ended June 30th, 1879, there were 135.02 inches of rainfall at Wilmington, N. C., 108.04 inches at Newport, R. I., 103.73 inches at Jacksonville, Fla., 86.36 inches at New York, and only 83.5 inches at Atlantic City.

"If it were desirable to prolong this article, I could cite numerous cases of consumption which have been markedly benefited by a winter's residence here. I can recall several persons who came here a few years ago with chronic cough and evidences of consolidation in part of one lung, and, having experienced decided improvement, have remained ever since, winter and summer. The disease in these cases seems to be arrested. The majority of such patients here are from Philadelphia and Pennsylvania, but within the last two or three years I have seen many consumptives from New York, as well as from Boston and other cities of New England. Some who came in the last stage found no benefit, but nearly all who have come while the disease was yet in an early stage, or, if further progressed, was pursuing a slow and chronic course, gained, at least, for a time.

"One notable case is that of a New York merchant who spent last winter here. After having had several hemorrhages and become considerably emaciated, he came here early in November, with instructions from his physicians to proceed farther south as soon as the weather grew too cold for him. He remained all winter, walking out almost daily, and returned to New York in the spring to resume his business, greatly improved in health.

HYGIENIC HINTS AND SANITARY PRECAUTIONS.

In an article contributed to the Philadelphia *Medical Bulletin*, for November, 1880, the same writer thus alluded to some important hygienic considerations:

"'The matter of diet here is not so important in winter as in summer. Errors in this respect are not then apt to be followed by such serious consequences. But it is safe to counsel all invalids to restrain the prodigious appetite they are almost sure to acquire soon after coming. Otherwise, constipation, headaches, and loss of appetite eventually result, showing that an overloaded stomach and embarrassed liver have struck work.

"It is a mistake to suppose that one cannot take cold at the seashore.

"It is necessary, then, that invalids here should take the usual precautions against being chilled. In the winter season, and on summer evenings, wraps of some kind are always in order out of doors, though usually they need not be heavy.

"As to exercise, while some is needed by the weakest invalids, even though only of a passive kind, such as massage by a manipulator, or rubbing by an ordinary attendant after the bath, there is commonly little danger that those able to walk shall not get enough. Many are inclined to take too much, owing to the extraordinary stimulant effects of the air, and need to be restrained, lest they exhaust their small stock of vitality as fast as it can be replenished. But this tendency is far less in winter than in summer, when the nightly hops and other multitudinous pleasures and dissipations keep the more impressionable visitors in a constant whirl of feverish excitement.

"There is, at this season, a restful air about not only the select cottage boarding-houses, but also the largest hotels, even when crowded as they are in February and March with the *élite* of the great cities. The tired brain-workers and exhausted devotees of fashion, equally with the convalescents and more chronic invalids, having come to rest and recuperate, go about it, generally, in a quiet, sensible way.

"One word, finally, as to medicinal treatment. For some cases the air alone is sufficient. Others get on famously with the air and the help of judicious bathing. Still others need medicines, and lose by having them stopped during their stay at the seashore. For these last, the tonic and alterative virtues of the air often furnish just the adjuvants necessary to accomplish the cure. The medicines which at home were nugatory or only half successful may succeed perfectly with the aid of the sea-air, when neither, alone, would be sufficient."

THE SUMMER CLIMATE OF ATLANTIC CITY.

Since Atlantic City has become celebrated as a winter resort, some of its new friends imagine that the weather must be excessively warm in summer. It is sufficient on this head to say that for twenty years the place was known and patronized almost exclusively as a refuge from the summer heat of the great cities, and that still its summer patronage is tenfold greater than that during the winter and spring. The mean temperature for July, 1879, 1880, 1881 and 1882, was 72.4 ; for August in the same years 72.0.

There are upwards of four hundred hotels and boarding-houses in Atlantic City, and they are rarely otherwise than full at the midsummer season.

www.ingramcontent.com/pod-product-compliance
Lightning Source LLC
Chambersburg PA
CBHW022001100426
42738CB00042B/1365